Highlights™

PuzzleMania®
Winter Puzzles

HIGHLIGHTS PRESS

Honesdale, Pennsylvania

CONTENTS

When you finish a puzzle, check it off √.
Good luck, and happy puzzling!

Do the Math

Hidden Pictures®

2

Wordplay

Poetry Break

A-Mazing!

Look Twice

Fun & Games

Arts & Crafts

Ice Team

The **Puzzlemania PowerPlays** just won the championship! One teammate was named Most Valuable Player. Use the players' jersey numbers to figure out who the MVP is.

- The sum of the two digits is either 8 or 9.
- If you switch the order of the digits, the new number would be 18 greater than it is now.

Illustrated by Daryll Collins

Cool Crossword

This crossword puzzle was made for cool customers. The answer to every clue has to do with things that are cold. See how many you know. Hurry, before things start melting!

Across

3 Winter footwear
6 It keeps your neck warm
7 Tree that does not change its color
9 They pull a famous sleigh
11 Antarctic bird
13 Tiny falling bits of ice
16 White relative of the grizzly (two words)
17 Powdery flakes from the sky

Down

1 House made of ice
2 Icy bits on window panes
4 Hockey shoe
5 Huge floating piece of ice
8 Santa's home (two words)
10 A powerful snowstorm
12 It hangs from a roof
14 Like a seal but with tusks
15 Gloves without fingers
16 Snowy road clearer

7

The Puck Stops Here

 Move 1 space down

 Move 1 space up

 Move 1 space right

 Move 1 space left

Syd is trying to score the game-winning goal. Can you help her find the right path to the net? The symbols will tell you which way to move.

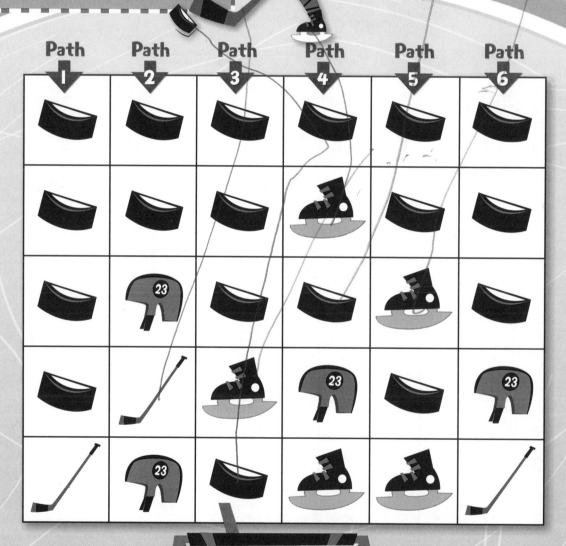

Illustrated by Scott Burroughs

8

Hidden Pictures®
A Winter Walk

Illustrated by Rocky Fuller

heart

arrow

flower

spoon

artist's brush

worm

comb

tooth

oven mitt

banana

pencil

scrub brush

carrot

football

Alaska Q's

Illustrated by Mike Moran   Puzzles by Carly Schuna

Doggone It!

Alaska's annual Iditarod Trail Sled Dog Race is about to start. But first Nick needs to figure out which one is his lead dog. Can you help him?

True or Not?

Which of these statements about Alaska are true and which are false?

1. Alaska was the 50th state to join the United States. **T or F**

2. Alaska's Mount McKinley (also known as Denali) is the highest mountain in the U.S. at just over 20,000 feet. **T or F**

3. Alaska is home to many minority groups called Alaska Natives, including Eskimos and Yupiks. **T or F**

4. Gazelles and lemurs are just a few of the species that are native to Alaska. **T or F**

5. Alaska has more land area than any other U.S. state. **T or F**

Moose Match

Can you find the two moose that look exactly alike?

ON Ice

Alaska is home to about half of the world's glaciers. You've been asked to make an ice carving to display at an annual Alaska ice festival. Draw your design here.

JUMBLed ANiMaLS

Unscramble each set of letters to get the name of an animal that lives in Alaska.

FLOW   — — — —

LESA   — — — —

NOSLAM   — — — — — —

LIZGRYZ ARBE   — — — — —

        — — — —

DALB GLEEA   — — — —

        — — — —

City or Not?

Each pair of words has one Alaskan city and one phony. Circle the cities.

Anchorage or **Assemblage?**

Fairpranks or **Fairbanks?**

Juniper or **Juneau?**

Rome or **Nome?**

Sitka or **Stanza?**

Tic Tac Row

Each of these snow globes has something in common with the other two snow globes in the same row. For example, in the first row across all three snow globes have ice rinks inside. Look at the other rows across, down, and diagonally. Can you tell what's alike in each row?

Letter Drop

Only six of the letters in the top line will work their way through this maze to land in the numbered squares at the bottom. When they get there, they will spell out the answer to the riddle.

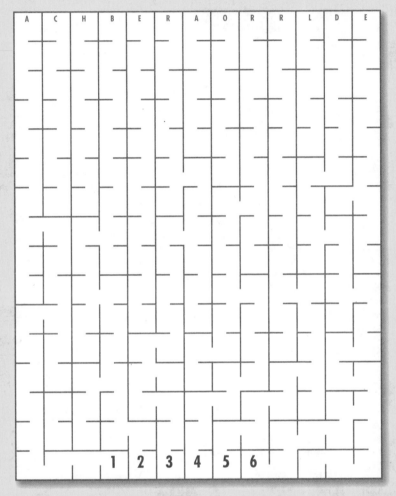

Top row letters: A C H B E R A O R R L D E

Bottom numbered squares: 1 2 3 4 5 6

What do you call a flamingo at the North Pole?

___ ___ ___ ___ ___ ___
 1   2   3   4   5   6

Illustrated by Jim Paillot

Get Down

Jack is about to tackle the toughest trail on the slopes. Can you help him find his way safely to the bottom of the mountain? Just one trail will take him there.

When you're done, write the letters you found along the route in order in the spaces below to see the answer to the riddle.

Why don't mountains get cold in the winter?

__ __ __ __ __ __ __ __ __ __ __ __ __ __ •

Illustrated by Steve Skelton

15

Seals and Walruses

Seals and Walruses is a strategy game for two players. The object of the game is to be the first player to get four of your pieces in a row, either across, down, or diagonally, on the other player's side of the board.

Equipment: Along with the board on the next page, you will need to supply your own game pieces, as well as a single die. There should be four seals and four walruses. The pieces can be buttons, coins, chips, or any other markers. Just be sure there are four pieces of one color and four pieces of another color, so you can tell the difference between the seals and the walruses.

Set up: Players may place their four pieces in any four of the boxes in the back row along their side.

To play: Both players roll the die. Highest number goes first.

A player may move any one piece the number shown on his or her die roll. The piece can move in any direction, either across, back, down, or diagonally, as long as all movement on any turn is in a straight line. Pieces may not enter or pass through a space that is occupied by any other piece. Also, a piece must move the total number shown on the die.

Players may block each other by moving their pieces next to the other player's row.

Players must always move one piece on a turn. Even if the only piece that can move will break up their own row, they still must move some piece. The only exception to this is if a player rolls a number, but all his or her pieces are blocked from going the full number either by the edge of the board or by the other player's pieces. In this case, the rolling player would forfeit his or her turn.

Remember, a player can win only if all four pieces are lined up on the other player's side of the board.

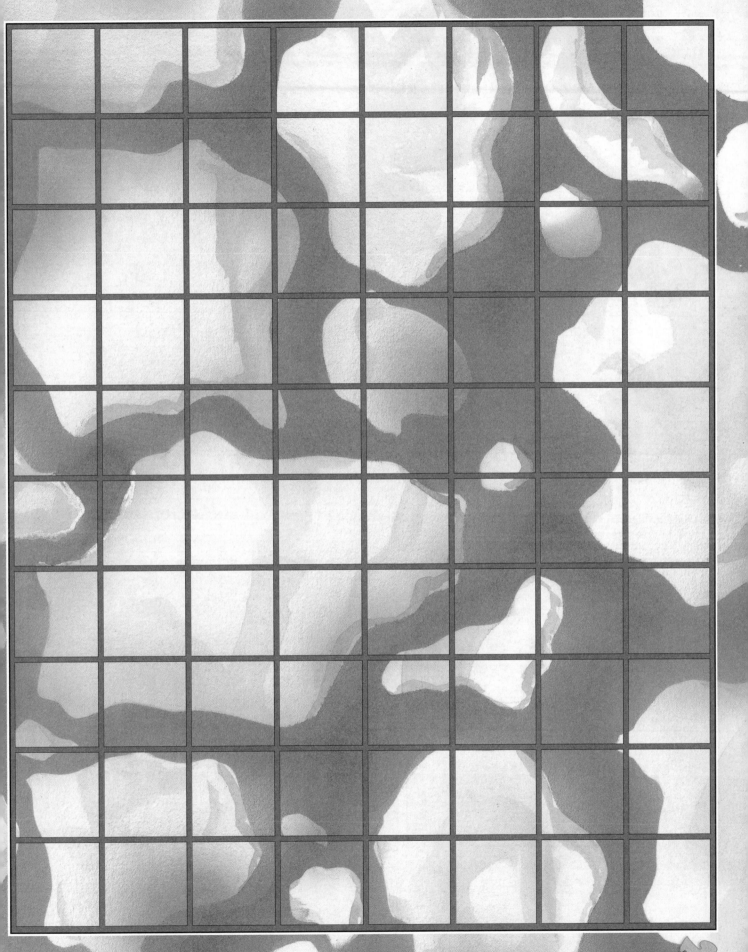

SQUARE Off!

Can you figure out what object appears in each picture? Unscramble the name of each.

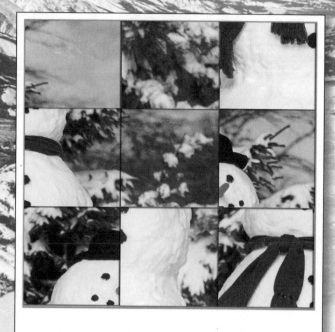

WONMASN

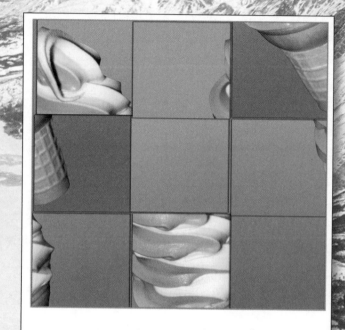

CEI-MACRE ONCE

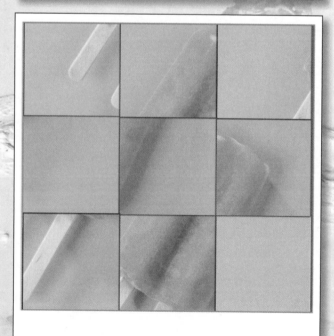

CEI OPP

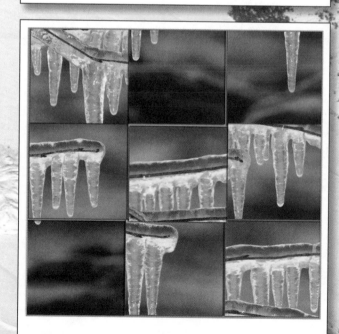

CLICIES

What do they all have in common?

sleet

By Rebecca J. Gomez
Art by Mike Litwin

Winter rain.
It bites and stings,
like frost-formed hornets
with ice-tipped wings.

To the Top

The Explorers Club held its second annual Trailblazer Contest. Expert climbers Jeanine, Brad, and Nate were finalists in the competition. To earn the top prize, each needed to blaze a trail

Illustrated by Scott Peck

DELAYS

JEANINE

1. Felt rock in left boot while stopped at Pebble Creek. Knot in shoelace caused 20-minute delay until she could remove the rock.

BRAD

1. Took a 30-minute detour at Pebble Creek, trying to find shallow spot to cross.

2. Found berry patch near Bear Claw Ledge. Took 10-minute break to nibble.

NATE

1. Took 10 minutes to find a replacement for his water bottle, which sprang a leak at the beginning of contest.

2. Bogged down for 30 minutes in a swampy area near Pebble Creek.

3. Lost a contact lens at Bear Claw Ledge. Finally found it after 20 minutes.

to the peak of Mount Majestic. From the times marked on the mountain and the list of delays, can you judge which climber was the first to reach Pinnacle Peak?

PINNACLE PEAK

BEARCLAW LEDGE

2 HOURS, 20 MINUTES

150 MINUTES

2 HOURS, 30 MINUTES

4 HOURS, 25 MINUTES

210 MINUTES

4 HOURS, 10 MINUTES

PEBBLE CREEK

2 HOURS, 45 MINUTES

200 MINUTES

2 HOURS

Jeanine

Brad

Nate

Can you find these 12 items hidden in this ice-skating picture?

teapot

piece of pie

stool

cactus

comb

penny

mushroom

car

fire hydrant

pen

slice of orange

baseball

Dot to Dot

Connect the dots from 1 to 32 to see someone else who likes the ice and snow.

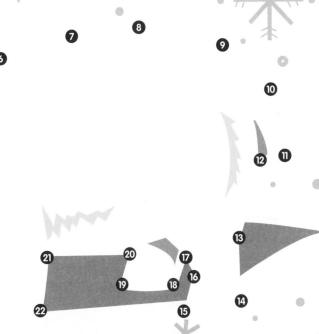

Illustrated by Dave Klug

Penguin Path

This penguin is hungry! Can you help him slip and slide down a path that leads into the water so he can fish for food? Be careful not to crash into any other penguins.

Start

Finish

Downhill Run

Can you tell who won this downhill race? All of the skiers made good time. (Each skier's flags are the same color as his or her nametag.) But the judges are subtracting points for every flag that a racer knocked over on the way down. Starting with the flag at the top of each skier's run, add or subtract the numbers on the next flag. Add the number when the flag is standing up, subtract the number when the flag is on the ground.

TRUDEE

MARA

JEAN

HERB

Illustrated by Anni Matsick

25

HOCKEY SEARCH

There are lots of hockey sticks at the pond toda

26

Can you find?

- 1 squirrel
- 2 scarves
- 3 hockey pucks
- 4 stars

Illustrated by Scott Burroughs

No-Snow Snowman

By Gretchen M. Everin

1. With an adult's permission, cut three 18-inch squares from old T-shirts.

2. To make a small "snowball," place the flat side of a full roll of toilet paper in the center of a T-shirt square. Tightly pull the fabric up and around the roll, then stuff the ends into the tube.

3. Make a medium snowball and a large one by padding two more rolls with plastic grocery bags before covering them with the T-shirt squares.

4. Cut slits in the bottom of the small and medium snowballs. Slide all three snowballs onto a ruler or dowel to hold them together.

5. For arms, cut two holes in the medium snowball. Insert twigs into the holes and glue them in place.

6. Add buttons, a hat, and a felt scarf and bird.

You Will Need:

- T-shirts
- toilet paper
- plastic grocery bags
- ruler
- dowel
- twigs
- buttons
- hat
- felt

More Ideas

Create other figures in this way. Make a clown by covering the body with pieces of multicolored tissue paper and decorating it with pompon buttons, a red nose, and yarn hair.

Make an ant by laying the body on its side and covering it with black tissue paper pieces. Add chenille-stick legs and antenna and paper eyes.

Snow Bank

By A.K. Pilenza

1. Cover a cardboard box with white cardstock.

2. Cut out a nose, mouth, eyes, earmuff strip, and other details from cardstock. Glue them on.

3. Ask an adult to cut a slit in the top of the box (to insert money) and a flap in the back (to remove it).

4. For earmuffs, cover two applesauce cups with felt. Glue them over the ends of the earmuff strip.

You Will Need:

- cardboard box
- cardstock
- applesauce cups
- felt

Valentine's Day "Fortune" Hearts

By Jan Fields

You Will Need:

- cardstock
- paper

1. Cut out a pair of hearts from cardstock. Glue the edges together.

2. Write a Valentine's Day "fortune" on a narrow strip of paper.

3. Cut the heart down the center, leaving a small connection at the point.

4. Glue the left side of the fortune into the left half of the heart. Fold the fortune and insert it into the right half of the heart.

5. Write a name on a small strip of paper. Glue it to the heart to hold the left and right sides together.

Silly Sledding

Hang on tight! There are some strange sights at the sledding hill today. Can you find at least **25** odd, weird, or wacky things in this picture?

Illustrated by Genevieve Kote

Slippery Slope

Whee! Bianca is about to head down the slope.
Can you help her ski safely to the bottom?

Start

Finish

STUCK IN THE ICE

Each of these 12 words has the letters **I-C-E** frozen to it. Skate through this puzzle by using the clues below to fill in the rest of the words.

1.  i c e
2.  i c e
3.  i c e
4.  i c e
5.  i c e
6.  i c e
7.  i c e
8.  i c e
9.  i c e
10.  i c e
12.  i c e   i c e

11.  i c e

1. This cereal grain is eaten by people all around the world.
2. Roll these in a game to see how many spaces to move.
3. It's the opposite of *nasty*.
4. These small, long-tailed animals are in the rodent family.
5. This is more than once, but less than three times.
6. This adds flavor to food.
7. Cut a piece from something.
8. This is what something costs.
9. Enjoy this drink made from fruit or vegetables.
10. You use this when you sing.
11. Other people may offer these words of wisdom.
12. This person's job is to enforce the law.

The 🔑 to It All

This puzzle holds many keys. Thirty-three words or phrases that contain the letters **KEY** are hidden in the grid. Each time **KEY** appears in a word, it is replaced by a 🔑. Look up, down, across, backwards, and diagonally to find the words. Then write the leftover letters that are not Xs in order from left to right and top to bottom to find the answer to the riddle.

Word List

~~CAR KEY~~
DONKEY
HAWKEYED
HOCKEY
HOKEY POKEY
HOUSE KEY
JOCKEY
JOKEY
KEYBOARD
KEY CARD
KEYHOLE

KEYNOTE
KEYPAD
KEYPUNCH
KEYRING
KEYSTONE
KEYSTROKE
KEYWORD
LACKEY
LATCHKEY
LOCKER KEY
MALARKEY

MASTER KEY
MONKEY
OFF-KEY
OKEYDOKEY
PASSKEY
POKEY
REKEY
SKELETON KEY
SOCKEYE SALMON
TURKEY
TURNKEY

34

X T J S K E L E T O N X G
M C X X O H E X O F F X N X
A A N T S S A P F X I L X
L L O W U O X X X R X R X
A X M O R X X H O L E X
R N L R D X H O N A R X
P A D X T H O C A R X D
I U S X H C X M H O D R
X N E D C D N O P A O R A
L C E T X A O X M C A O
O H C E A L X T X S O B
C X O W L X X E X T R T
K A S A X K X E R U X E
E E R H J X U X X X
R X X T N O M R S T O N C X
T S T R O K E E S U O H C X
Y X O T D O T S H O P O

Match Maker

Every snazzy sock in the picture has one that looks just like it.
Find all 10 matching pairs.

Illustrated by Dave Joly

Snow Problem

Jasmine is shoveling snow from driveways to make some extra money. She charges people by the length of the property that she shovels. Can you use the information below to help her figure out the length of a house lot and a parking lot? (Hint: The information tells you how long a driveway is. Use that to figure out the length of a house lot.)

Three house lots and one driveway are as long as a parking lot.
Two driveways are as long as one house lot.
A parking lot is seven times longer than a driveway.
Three and one-half house lots will fit into a parking lot.
Each driveway is 100 feet long.

Illustrated by R. Michael Palan

Hidden Pictures®
Double Fun

snake

hatchet

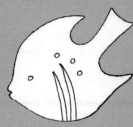
fish

spoon

slice of cake

ice-cream cone

slice of bread

handbell

wishbone

glass

pliers

Illustrated by Olivia Cole

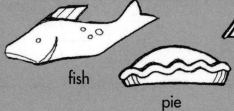
fish

pie

book

carrot

teacup

slice of pizza

mushroom

39

Snow Day!

C'mon down and join the fun! Before these friends reach the bottom of the hill, see if you can find at least **20** differences between these pictures.

Which two sleds look exactly alike?

Illustrated by Kevin Rechin

Can you find these 12 items hidden at this maple-sugar harvest?

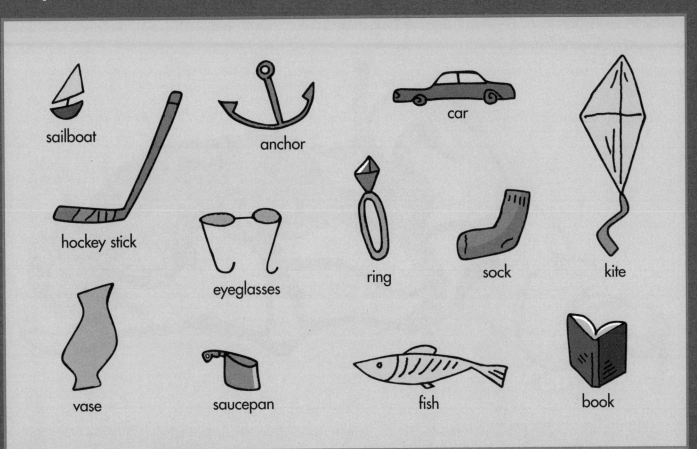

sailboat

anchor

car

hockey stick

eyeglasses

ring

sock

kite

vase

saucepan

fish

book

Dot to Dot

Connect the dots from 1 to 35
to see a sight from the woods.

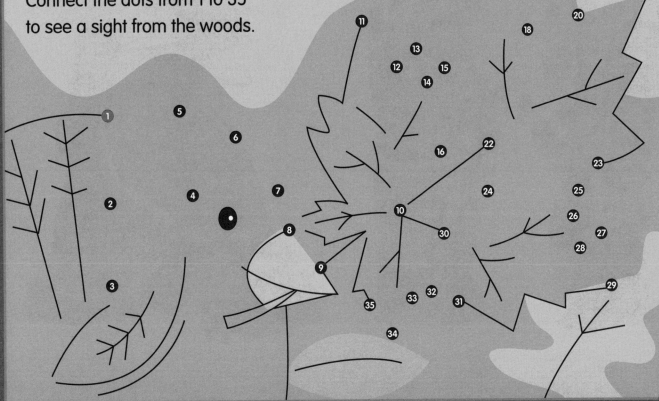

Illustrated by Dave Klug

43

These winter things have been twisted and turned.
Can you figure out what each one is?

45

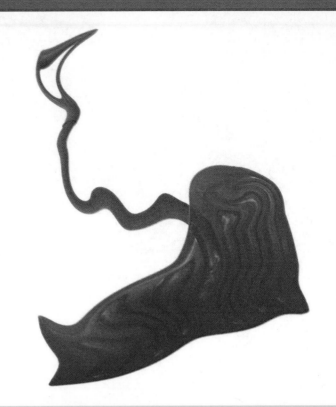

Precise Ice

See if you can trace this figure without crossing over or doubling back on any lines.

Illustrated by Barbara Gray

PLOW A PATH

The Hardwood County Commissioners need to conserve gas for their snow plow. Can you find a path that covers each road exactly once? The plow is parked in Maple City, so the route you choose should start and end there.

Oakville

Lumber Rest

Wooddale

Maple City

Walnut Crossing

Ashton

Twin Branch

Cherry Grove

Twice the Ice

This rink is a hot spot! While everyone goes around and around, see if you can uncover at least **20** differences between these pictures.

Which one of these people is not at the rink today?

49

SNOW BALL

Up in Barrow, Alaska, more than 60 percent of the people have Inuit roots. They live with white flakes so much of the year that they use specific words to describe different types of snow. In fact, no one seems to know exactly how many of these words there really are.

Nineteen of these snow words are hidden in this grid. Look forward, backward, up, down, and diagonally to find them.

WORDS FOR SNOW

AKELRORAK (newly drifting snow)

ANIUK (snow for melting into water)

ANIUVAK (snowbank)

APINGAUT (first snowfall)

APUN (snow)

AUKSALAK (melting snow)

AYAK (snow on clothes)

KATIKSUNIK (light snow)

KIKSRUKAK (glazed snow in a thaw)

MASSAK (snow and water)

MAVSA (snowdrift overhead)

MITAILAK (soft snow over an ice floe)

NATIGVIK (snowdrift)

NUTAGAK (powder snow)

PERKSERTOK (drifting snow)

POKAKTOK (salt-like snow)

PUKAK (sugar snow)

SILLIK (hard, crusty snow)

SISUUK (avalanche)

M L S K A K U R S K I K
I A P I N G A U T G K K
U A U E S R E P A O A R
K Y K U I U K E N T L P
A A A E L R U R I O I O
G U K A L A S K U A A K
A P U N I R S S V Y T A
T M O S K U O E A A I K
U A T A N L L R K K M T
N V K I V G I T A N T O
R S K L I L N O S K I K
P A M A S S A K U I N A

"You'll have to walk up the hill now.
I need the ski lift."

51

Knit It

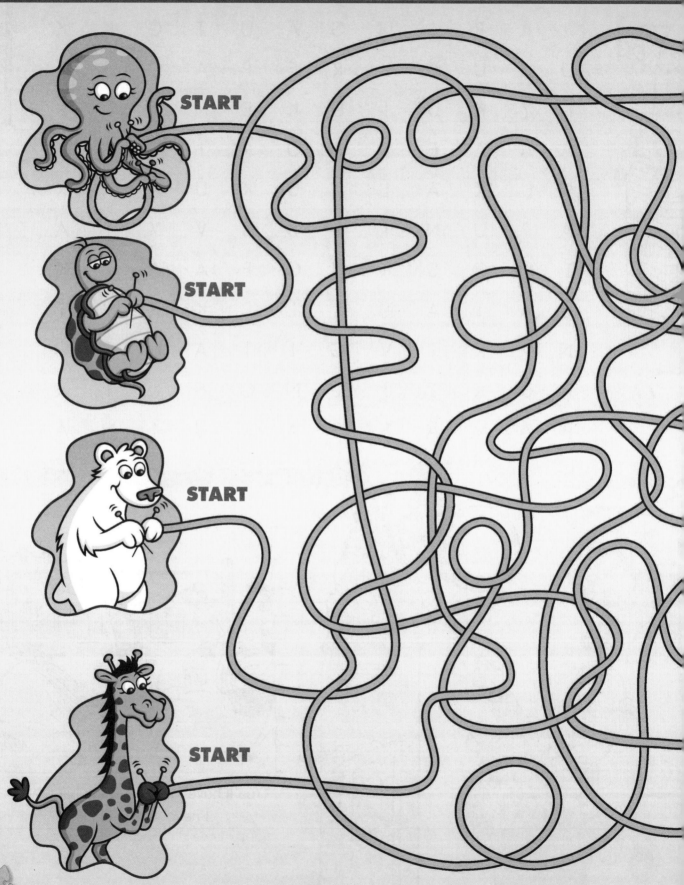

START

START

START

START

52

Look at those knitting needles go!
Follow the yarn trails to see what each animal is making.

Illustrated by Sean Parkes

Snow Way!

Simon and three of his friends shoveled snow for money. Each used some of his or her earnings to buy something. From the clues below, can you tell what each friend bought and how much it cost?

Use the chart to keep track of your answers. Put an **X** in each box that can't be true and an **O** in boxes that match.

	Video Game	Sweater	Art Supplies	Basketball	$50	$35	$30	$25
Simon								
Nora								
Oscar								
Wanda								

1. Nora's art supplies cost more than Oscar's item, but less than Wanda's.
2. Simon bought the only piece of clothing.
3. Wanda's item cost twice as much as Oscar's.
4. The sweater cost more than the art supplies, but the video game cost more than the sweater.

Wish for
a Mouse

By Eileen Spinelli
Art by Robert Crawford

Scurrying mouse,

be blessed.

Find silken ribbon

for your nest,

forgotten grain

beneath the snow,

and shelter

when the owl

flies low.

Snow Biz

After a day on the slopes, it's time to head back to the lodge to relax. But there are some strange sights outside the ski lodge tonight. Can you find at least **25** odd, weird, or wacky things in this picture?

Illustrated by Dave Clegg

Can you find these 12 items hidden at this sledding hill?

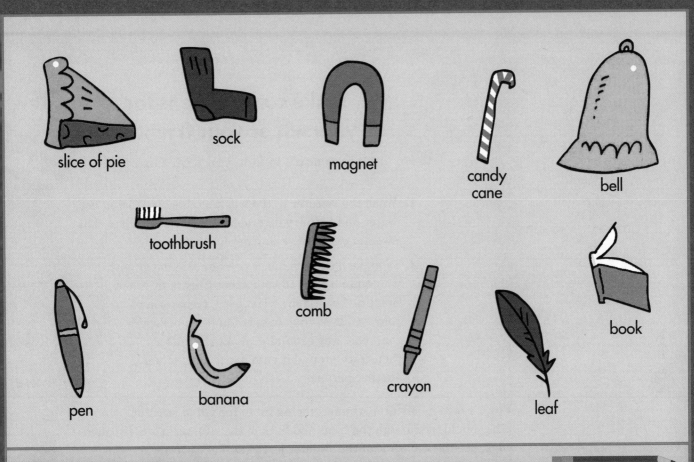

slice of pie

sock

magnet

candy cane

bell

toothbrush

comb

book

pen

banana

crayon

leaf

Dot to Dot

Connect the dots from 1 to 33 to see someone else who likes the cold.

Illustrated by Dave Klug

Easy Felted Mittens

By Thelma Godin

You will need:
- an old 100-percent-wool sweater (not angora) that a parent will let you use (if you don't have one, you might find one at a secondhand store)
- laundry detergent, washing machine, and dryer
- paper
- pencil
- ruler
- scissors
- straight pins
- yarn
- large-eyed needle

Make cozy mittens for yourself or your friends.

Ask an adult to help you with this craft.

1. Wash the sweater in the washing machine, using hot water and laundry detergent. Dry it in the dryer. The sweater will shrink and become felted.

2. To make a pattern, place one hand on paper with your thumb out and your other fingers together. Starting below your wrist bone, trace around your hand, leaving an extra half inch of space the whole way around. Cut out the pattern, then trace around it onto paper and cut out another pattern.

Tip: Mix colors and patterns of different sweaters!

3. Pin the mitten patterns, thumbs facing in, to the felted sweater. The pins should go through the front and back of the sweater. For a finished edge, use the waistline of the sweater as the cuff of each mitten. Cut around the patterns through both layers of the sweater.

4. Remove the paper patterns. For each mitten, pin the sweater pieces together, matching the thumbs.

5. Thread a large-eyed needle with a 6-foot-long piece of yarn. Make a large knot at the end.

6. Beginning near the cuff of one mitten, push the needle through both layers and around the edge. A short distance from the first stitch, push the needle through again. Stitch all the way around the mitten.
Don't sew the mitten shut!

6 feet long

knot

7. Tie a large knot at the cuff, and trim the excess yarn. Be sure to remove all the pins.

8. Repeat steps 5, 6, and 7 to make the second mitten.

Hockey Hunt

You circle, you score! We've hidden **24** ice-hockey words in this grid. Look for them up, down, across, backwards, and diagonally. Now go shoot for the goal!

Word List

- ~~ASSIST~~
- BLUE LINE
- CHECKING
- CREASE
- DEFENSE
- DROP PASS
- FACE-OFF
- GOALIE
- HAT TRICK
- HIGH-STICKING
- ICING
- NET
- OFFENSE
- OFF SIDES
- PENALTY BOX
- POWER PLAY
- PUCK
- RINK
- SAVE
- SCORE
- SKATES
- SLAP SHOT
- SLASHING
- ZONE

```
H S R E S S A P P O R D P
I G I F A C E O F F T C E
G L N C E T E N G F O H N
H O K R B V Y O I E H E A
S F G E G I A W C N S C L
T F E A N L L S I S P K T
I S N S I Q P N N E A I Y
C I I E H S R G G O L N B
K D L E S N E F E D S G O
I E E R A O W T A E J G X
N S U O L L O D A R N A C
G Y L C S O P U C K Y O R
W U B S T S I S S A S Y Z
T H A T T R I C K G Y F P
```

61

Time for a Nap

This bear is sleepy. Help him find a clear path from **START** to **FINISH** so he can take a long nap.

FINISH

Illustrated by Sean Parkes

Weather Q's

Snow Tread

Charlotte's town is covered in snow! Can you help her find the one path home from school?

Start

Finish

Illustrated by Mike Moran   Puzzles by Carly Schuna

Weather Quiz

Which of these weather facts are true and which are false?

1. The longest lightning bolt ever recorded was nearly 120 miles long.

T or F

2. The hottest temperature ever recorded on the earth was in New Mexico.

T or F

3. The coldest temperature ever recorded on Earth was -50 degrees Fahrenheit.

T or F

4. The strongest wind gust ever recorded on the earth's surface was in New Hampshire.

T or F

Wacky Weather

Explorers have just discovered Climatopia—a place that has all four seasons on the same block! Draw a scene from Climatopia here.

Cloud Gazing

Three of these words are types of clouds, and the others are fakers. Can you circle the clouds?

RUMPUS

DIPLODOCUS

NIMBUS

ONUS

ABACUS

STRATUS

ESOPHAGUS **HIBISCUS**

CUMULUS

It's Raining, It's Pouring

Which two umbrellas match exactly?

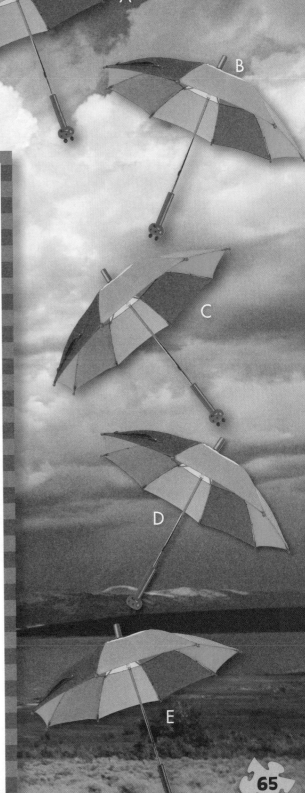

A

B

C

D

E

Weather Words

Meteorology is the study of weather and forecasting. It includes a huge number of topics—and a lot of words, too. Can you make at least **20** words from the letters in **METEOROLOGY**?

_____ _____

_____ _____

_____ _____

_____ _____

_____ _____

_____ _____

_____ _____

_____ _____

_____ _____

_____ _____

Silly Skill Hill

Illustrated by Sean Parkes

Rustic Log Cabin

You're the architect! Design a house, roll up some paper logs, and create a log cabin.

1. From cardboard, draw and cut out four walls with tabs. Each wall should have two tabs, one at the top of the left side and one at the bottom of the left side. Cut holes in the walls for windows and doors.

2. To make windows, cut squares from the window of a bakery box. Use a marker to draw panes. Tape the windows behind the cut-out window holes on the walls.

3. Put glue on the front of the tabs, and assemble the walls, with the tabs inside the cabin. To make each "log," cut a strip from a paper bag, roll it around a pencil, and glue the edges. Glue the logs on the walls. Let the end of every second log stick out to interlock with the logs from the other walls, as shown in the photo.

4. From cardboard, cut out a roof to fit the cabin. Glue it on. Make a chimney from cardboard. Cut the bottom to fit the angle of the roof. Glue it on. Glue the cabin on a piece of cardboard. Add details with a marker. Add a porch roof and other details with cardboard and paper rolls.

Then make a woodland setting, complete with a lake and trees.

You Will Need:

- grocery bags
- corrugated cardboard
- scissors
- bakery box with a plastic window
- markers
- tape and glue
- pencil
- plastic drinking straws
- paints
- sand

To Make the Trees

Cut a long, 3-inch-wide strip from a bag. Draw a line diagonally across it. Cut fringe on one side of the line. Starting with the end with the short fringe, wrap the strip around a plastic straw, gluing it and bending out the fringe as you go. Tape down the end. Cut a square from cardboard and cut a slit in the middle. Insert the straw end through the slit, cut the end in half vertically, and tape the two straw parts to the cardboard.

To Make the Lake

Cut out a lake shape from a paper bag. Paint it, leaving the beach section unpainted. Spread glue on the beach section and sprinkle sand on it. Let it dry. Create a dock by gluing paper logs onto a piece of cardboard.

More Ideas

Adapt the rolled-paper technique to add a 3-D effect to other crafts. Decorate a photo frame or a pencil can to look wooden by gluing on rolled paper-bag strips.

FLAKE SEARCH

This party is covered in snowflakes!

70

Can you find?

Two of the snowflakes are the same. Can you find them?

Illustrated by Scott Burroughs

Hidden Pictures® Snow Kidding

There is more than meets the eye on this slope.
Can you find the hidden objects?

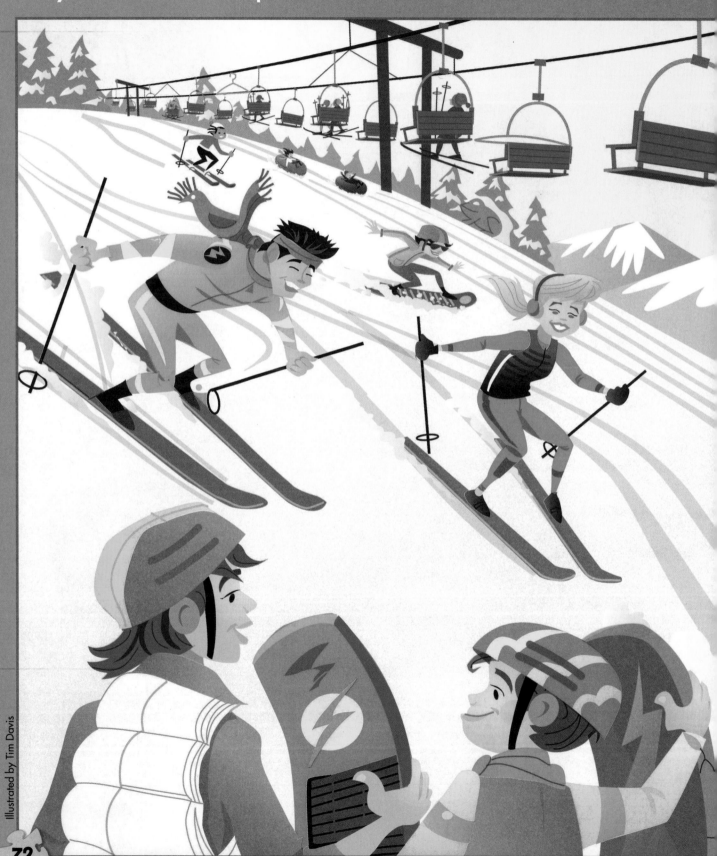

Illustrated by Tim Davis

open book

crown

bottle

frog

paper clip

glove

hanger

goose

heart

fish

ice-cream cone

bird

saiboat

candle

bell

comb

baseball cap

tweezers

bat

star

banana

slice of bread

needle

saw

BABY BEAR RIDDLE

Riddle: Why were the baby bears cold, even under the warmest quilt?

To answer the riddle, circle the letters in the quilt squares that have dots. Print your circled letters in order in the spaces below. Then find the matching quilt squares.

——— ——— ——— ——— ——— ——— ——— ———

——— ——— ——— ——— ———   ——— ——— ——— ——— ———.

Illustrated by Carolyn D. Conahan

Hidden Pictures®
Dog Sleds

tic-tac-toe

mushroom

fried egg

crescent moon

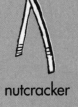

bowl

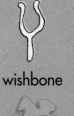

nutcracker

shoelace

comb

spoon

needle

candle

yo-yo

lollipop

wishbone

Illustrated by George Wildman

Slide to the Finish

START

Illustrated by Ron Zalme

FINISH

77

Every sweater in the picture has one that looks just like it. Find all 10 matching pairs.

79

The Right Route

It's Groundhog Day, and Phil is late for his big appearance. Can you help him find the path to the top? Only one route will take you there. Don't get grounded along the way!

Finish
FeBRUARY
2
ZZZ
Start

Illustrated by Jim Paillot

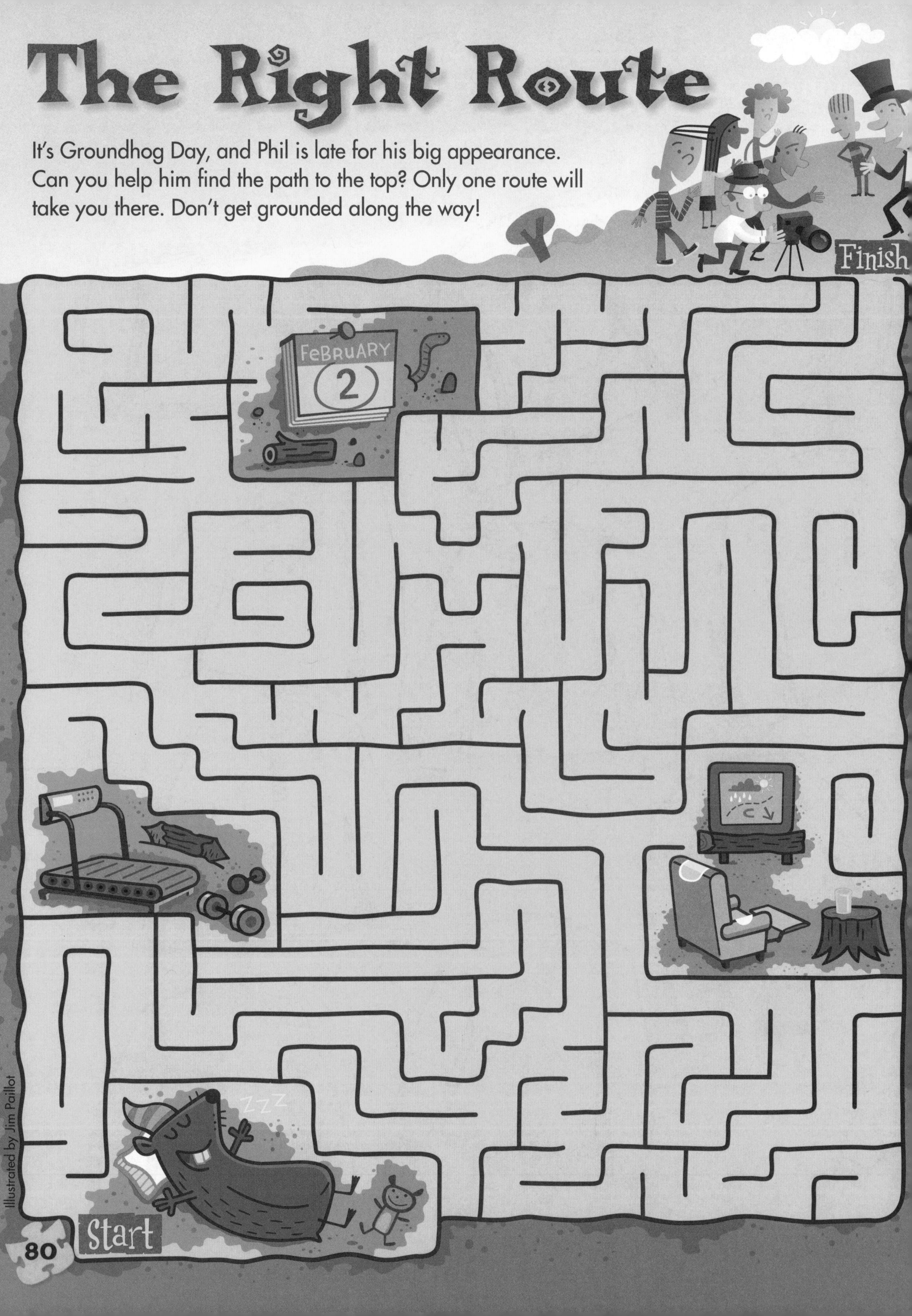

Mental Blocks

Arrange each set of words into its block. You'll use each word only once. When you're done, each block will have words reading across in each row and down in each column. We've filled in the first word to get you started. Can you fill in the rest?

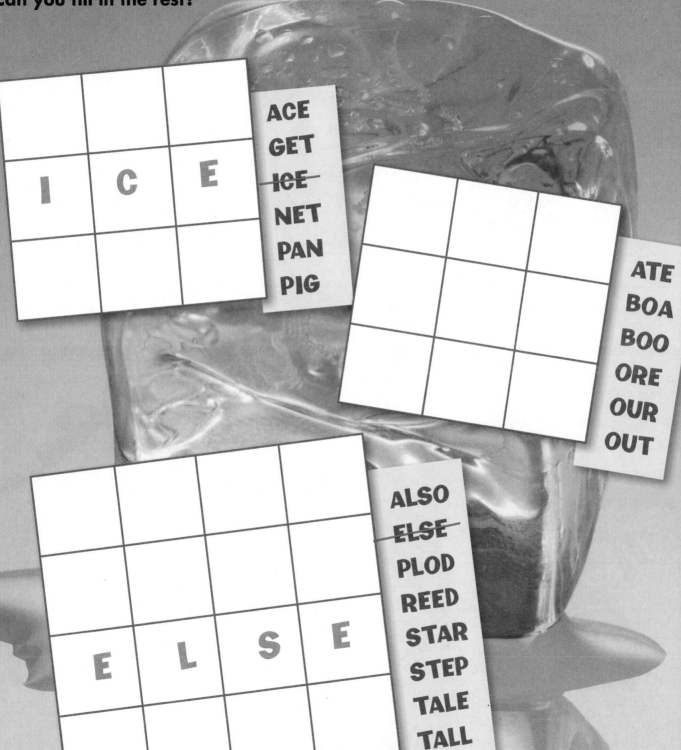

ACE
GET
~~ICE~~
NET
PAN
PIG

ATE
BOA
BOO
ORE
OUR
OUT

ALSO
~~ELSE~~
PLOD
REED
STAR
STEP
TALE
TALL

Puzzle by Janet Hammond

Can you find these 12 items hidden in this winter scene?

comb

watering can

ghost

crayon

ruler

light bulb

paintbrush

hotdog

bowling pin

high-heeled shoe

saltshaker

key

Dot to Dot

Connect the dots from 1 to 35 to see something that will warm you up.

I ♥ Cookies

Amy's class is enjoying their big Valentine's Day party. To add to the fun, someone played matchmaker with the cookies! Each cookie on Amy's tray has one exact match somewhere in the room. Can you find all six matches?

Illustrated by Mike Moran

85

To My Valentine

If apples were pears,
And peaches were plums,
And the rose had a different name;
If tigers were bears,
And fingers were thumbs,
I'd love you just the same!

—*Anonymous*

Peak Performance

Cleo planted a flag at the top of Mount Mammoth. It's your job to place a number in that flag. Start at the bottom. Add the numbers on two flags and place the sum in the flag above them. Keep going till you reach the top.

71

27 44 31 19

The Amazing Mazers

ADVENTURES UP NORTH

Mrs. Martinelli and her mail chopper are missing! The Frozen Face, Alaska, Post Office has wired the Amazing Mazers for help.

Over the radio, we heard her cry, "Oh, a screw has fallen off!" Then "There goes a spring." After that there were eleven more muffled cries. Next we heard a swoosh and then silence.

"Mush, mush," cry Millie and Max to Master and his mates as they get hot on the trail. But which way should they go to find the helicopter in the snow?

Help the Mazers follow the trail of **thirteen** dropped chopper objects that will lead to Mrs. Martinelli. Use your eyes and listen for cries. Every ice-packed moment counts.

This is a real mush rush!

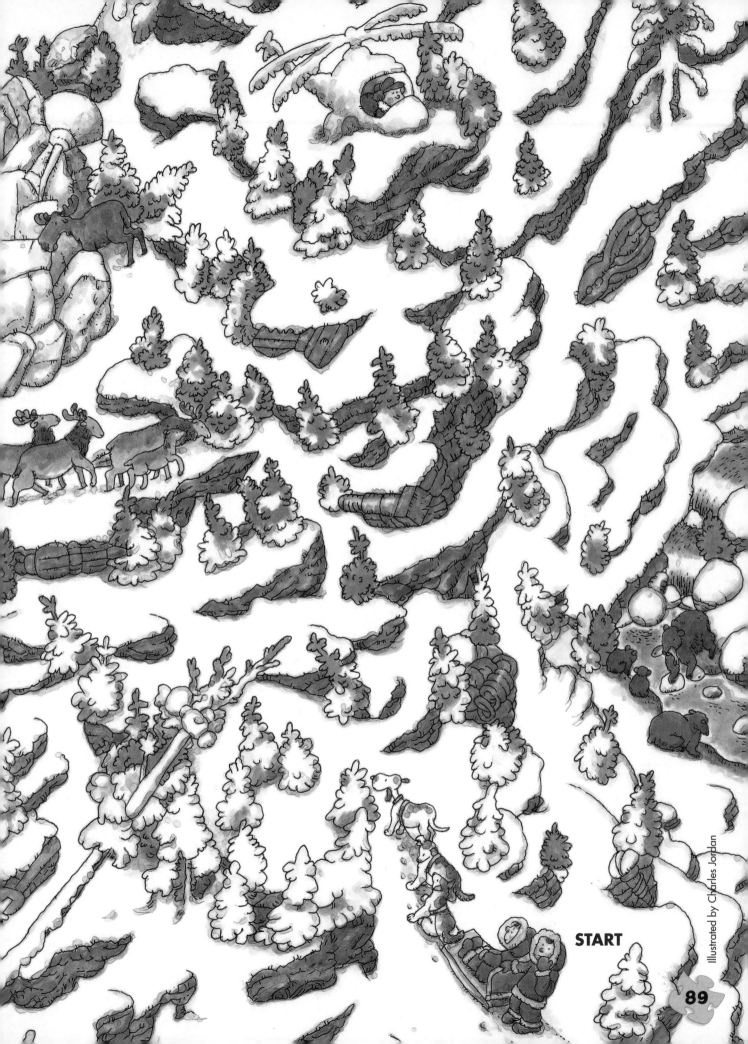

START

89

Hidden Pictures®
Waiting for a Nibble

funnel

comb

magnet

crescent moon

mallet

needle

spoon

nail

ruler

hat

mitten

envelope

canoe

Illustrated by Rocky Fuller

Two of a Kind

Can you find the two snowmen that are the same?

Illustrated by Clay Cantrell

Crafts

Cupid's Arrows Game

By April Theis

1. Cut out a large heart from poster board. Decorate it.
2. Draw 16 spaces along the edge. In two spaces, write "Give an Arrow." In three spaces, write "Take an Arrow." In four spaces, write "Cupid." Write "Start," as shown.
3. For the spinner, cut an arrow and a circle from cardstock. Draw six sections. Secure a fastener through the arrow, circle, and game board.
4. Glue paper arrowheads and "feathers" onto 15 straws. For Cupid's quiver, cover a can with paper. Glue on a paper handle.
5. For each 3-D game piece, cut three hearts from paper. Fold them in half. Glue a side of one heart to the side of another heart. Glue the third heart to the remaining two sides.

You Will Need:
- poster board
- cardstock
- fastener
- paper
- straws
- can

To Play:

Place three arrows in Cupid's quiver. Give each player three arrows. Taking turns, players spin, then move their game pieces. If they land on "Cupid," they put an arrow into Cupid's quiver. For "Take an Arrow," they take an arrow from the quiver. For "Give an Arrow," they give an arrow to another player. The first person to get rid of all of his or her arrows wins!

Groundhog Day Door Hanger

By Michelle Budzilowicz

1. Cut a rectangle from thin cardboard. Ask an adult to cut a doorknob hole near the top.

2. Use paper and markers to create a sunny scene on one side and a cloudy scene on the other. Use a layer of paper to create a pocket on each side.

3. Cut out a groundhog from thin cardboard. Add details with markers.

4. If there will be six more weeks of winter, put the groundhog in the pocket on the sunny side. If spring weather is coming early, put him on the cloudy side.

You Will Need:

- thin cardboard
- paper
- markers

Chef's Hat

By Lynne Marie Pisano

1. Cut two wide strips from paper. Tape the ends together so the paper fits your head.

2. Tape a large square of tissue paper to the inside edge of the headband so that it creates a pouf. Trim the excess tissue paper.

You Will Need:

- paper
- tissue paper

Arctic Animals

Here in the frozen North, residents solve puzzles to pass the time. To find these Arctic answers, use the letter square. For each blank, find the row with the matching shape.

	1	2	3	4	5
🧢	V	W	X	Y	Z
🐟	A	E	I	M	R
🔥	B	F	J	N	S
🧤	C	G	K	O	T
🧊	D	H	L	P	U

1. This animal has flat, hairy feet designed for walking over wet tundra or snow. It may travel in large groups of up to 100,000 members.

2. This animal digs into the ground in the summer to hide food. Because the ground is always partly frozen, it acts as a handy icebox. One scientist discovered 105 bird carcasses hidden in one hole.

Then go across to find the matching numbered column. Find the letter where the row meets the column. Write the letter on the blank to put this puzzle on ice.

3. This animal has almost transparent eyelids that work like sunglasses. The eyelids protect the eyes from the sun's glare.

___4 ___4 ___3 ___1 ___5   ___1 ___2 ___1 ___5

4. During icy winter storms, this bird digs a little burrow, where it stays warm and protected.

___4 ___5 ___1 ___5 ___4 ___3 ___2 ___1 ___4

5. This animal grows an enormous second claw under the ones it is born with. This second claw may help it to shovel snow out of the way.

___5 ___4 ___4 ___2   ___3 ___2 ___4 ___4 ___3 ___4 ___2

Illustrated by David Helton

Hidden Pictures®
Snow Bears

carrot

pear

pencil

banana

hat

crown

canoe

pitcher

bird

grass skirt

fork

comb

fish

mitten

Illustrated by Unada Gliewe

Cookie Code

Ten kinds of cookies are listed here. It's up to you to crack the code and fill in the names. Each number stands for a different letter. Once you know one number's letter, you can fill in that letter in all of the words. Grab some milk and get started!

1. M A C A R O O N
   7 10 1 10 11 2 2 8

2. ___ ___ ___ ___ ___ ___ ___
   6 5 7 2 8 9 10 11

3. ___ ___ ___ ___ ___
   13 18 12 10 11

4. ___ ___ ___ ___ ___ ___ ___
   19 2 11 16 18 8 5

5. ___ ___ ___ ___ ___ ___ ___ ___ ___ ___
   12 4 8 12 5 11 13 8 10 14

6. ___ ___ ___ ___ ___ ___ ___ ___ ___
   13 15 2 11 16 9 11 5 10 17

7. ___ ___ ___ ___ ___ ___ ___ ___ ___ ___ ___ ___ ___
   2 10 16 7 5 10 6 11 10 4 13 4 8

8. ___ ___ ___ ___ ___ ___ ___ ___ ___ ___ ___ ___
   14 5 10 8 18 16 9 18 16 16 5 11

9. ___ ___ ___ ___ ___ ___ ___ ___ ___ ___ ___ ___ ___
   1 15 2 1 2 6 10 16 5 1 15 4 14

10. ___ ___ ___ ___ ___ ___ ___ ___ ___ ___ ___ ___ ___
    13 8 4 1 3 5 11 17 2 2 17 6 5

BONUS PUZZLE

Did you fill in all the names? Use the same code to answer this riddle.

What did the gingerbread man use to trim his fingernails?

___ ___ ___ ___ ___ ___ ___ ___ ___ ___ ___ ___
10 1 2 2 3 4 5 1 18 16 16 5 11

97

Every winter hat in the picture has one that looks just like it.
Find all 10 matching pairs.

Ice Escapades

Illustrated by Sean Parkes

Wrapping Up

Eli's friends surprised him with a birthday party and presents. But they forgot to put tags on the gifts. Using the clues below, can you figure out which friend gave Eli which gift?

Use the chart to keep track of your answers. Put an **X** in each box that can't be true and an **O** in boxes that match.

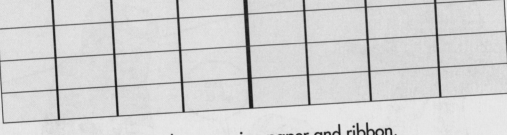

	Red Gift	Blue Gift	Yellow Gift	Green Gift	Red Bow	Blue Bow	Yellow Bow	Green Bow
Amber								
Billy								
Chad								
Daphne								

1. No gift has the same color wrapping paper and ribbon.
2. A girl brought a yellow gift with a red bow.
3. Billy did not put a green bow on his gift.
4. Amber did not bring a red bow or gift.
5. Billy used his favorite color, blue, to wrap his gift.

Puzzle by Cynthia Elam

Bunny Run

Help the bunny slalom down the hill and cross the finish line.

FINISH

HEART SEARCH

This Valentine's Day party has a lot of hearts.

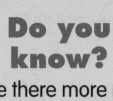

Do you know?

Are there more red or white hearts in the picture?

Hidden Pictures On Ice

There is more than meets the eye at this skating rink.
Can you find the hidden objects?

Illustrated by Peter Grosshauser

heart

canoe

snake

slice of pizza

feather

spoon

clover

fishhook

balloon

plate

carrot

rocket

flashlight

ladybug

suitcase

red pepper

test tube

fork

spatula

paper clip

cookie

ring

party hat

comb

question mark

fish

mallet

107

Sleep Walk

It's time to hibernate! Can you help this bear find the one path to her cave? Hurry, before she falls asleep.

YAWN

Start

Finish

XING

Accidental Memories Part 1

Take a long look at this picture. Try to remember everything you see. Then turn the page, and try to answer some questions about this scene without looking back.

Illustrated by C. Murphy

DON'T READ THIS UNTIL YOU HAVE LOOKED AT "Accidental Memories-Part 1" ON PAGE 109.

Accidental Memories **Part 2**

Try to answer these questions without looking back at the scene. Follow the directions and place certain letters in the numbered spaces at the bottom. If you're a good eyewitness and remember everything correctly, you'll answer the riddle in no time.

1. What name was on the coffee mug?
   If it was Ed, put an O in space 9.
   If it was Dad, put an I in space 4.

2. What broke the window?
   If it was a baseball, put a T in space 8.
   If it was a snowball, put a T in space 3.

3. How many people were wearing hats?
   If fewer than three, put an N in space 10.
   If more than three, put an N in space 7.

4. How many cats were in the room?
   If one, put an R in space 5.
   If two, put a D in space 5.

5. Was anyone walking under the ladder?
   If yes, put an L in space 8.
   If no, put an L in space 10.

6. What color paint was being spilled?
   If red, put an X in space 2.
   If green, put a W in space 1.

7. Was there a screen over the fireplace?
   If no, put an E in spaces 3 and 6.
   If yes, put an E in spaces 4 and 7.

8. What was showing on the television?
   If it was a weather report, put an A in spaces 1 and 9.
   If it was a sports report, put an A in space 2.

What kind of clinic would a lumberjack visit for a toothache?

An __ __ __ __ __ __ __ __ __ __ clinic
   1 2 3 4 5 6 7 8 9 10

Illustrated by C. Murphy

What's Next?

These pictures are out of order. For example, C happened first.
Can you figure out the logical order for the rest?

Illustrated by Bill Basso

III

Snow Going

START

112

These dog-sled teams are ready to race!
Follow each path to find out which team slides into first, second, and third place.

113

Hidden Pictures® Valentine Cards

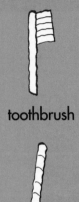

toothbrush

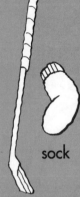

golf club

sock

key

sailboat

teacup

candle

flying disk

paintbrush

muffin

worm

tack

caterpillar

book

Illustrated by David Helton

Box Out

Follow the directions to cross out certain boxes. When you're done, write the remaining letters in order from left to right and top to bottom. They will give you the answer to the riddle.

Cross out all numbers divisible by **4**.
Cross out all numbers divisible by **7**.

A	T	M	M	C	A
18	8	35	35	37	12
R	M	O	E	C	A
21	16	22	28	63	52
L	C	I	T	L	O
32	17	48	36	70	30
R	F	D	A	A	Y
56	60	7	54	80	40
N	J	W	B	U	F
58	4	20	72	46	77
E	K	T	H	D	S
14	42	59	64	44	49

What do you call someone who is crazy about hot chocolate?

__ __ __ __ __ – __ __ __

On Boards

Ben finally caught up to Natalie at the bottom of the slope. While he catches his breath, see if you can find at least **20** differences between these pictures.

Which of these is **not** a real snowflake?

Illustrated by Tim Haggerty

Wiggle Pictures

These cold-weather animals have been twisted and turned.
Can you figure out what each one is?

Crafts

Juggle These Maracas!
By Sue Shadle

1. Put a handful of **beads**, **buttons**, or **beans** in a **plastic snack cup**.

2. Line the rim of the cup with **tacky glue**.

3. Press a matching snack cup upside down on top of the first cup. Let the glue dry.

4. Repeat steps 1 through 3 to make two more juggling balls.

This Mexican Tin Art Shines
By Chante McCoy

1. Use **permanent markers** to draw and decorate an animal shape on the bottom of a **disposable aluminum pie tin**.

2. Cut out the shape.

3. Punch a hole through the shape, and add a loop of **yarn** for a hanger.

Turn a Doorknob into a Snowman's Nose
By Kathy Ross

1. For the snowman's head, glue together two **paper plates** to make one sturdy plate.

2. In the center of the plate, cut two 4-inch slits in the shape of an X to allow the plate to slip over a doorknob.

3. Glue **cotton balls** on the front of the plate to cover it. Glue on **construction-paper** eyes and a mouth.

4. Cut out a hat from construction paper, and decorate it with **ribbon** or **fabric** trim. Staple it to the plate.

5. For a scarf, fringe the ends of a fabric strip, and staple it to the bottom of the snowman's head.

Snowflake Trivet

By Jean Kuhn

1. With an adult's help, take apart eight **spring-type clothespins**. Discard the springs.

2. Glue together the flat sides of two clothespin halves. Repeat with the others. **Paint** them.

3. Cut a 1½-inch circle from **thin cardboard**. Arrange and glue the clothespins so that the ends meet on the cardboard circle.

4. Decorate the snowflake with **glitter glue**.

Pinecone Snowman

By Merle J. Petersen

1. Use a **wooden skewer** to stuff bits of **cotton ball** between the scales of a **pinecone**.

2. With an adult's permission, cut the cuff off a **small sock**. Place the cuff on the pinecone as a hat. Tie the top with **yarn**, and cut fringe.

3. Glue on mittens cut from **felt**, a **chenille-stick** nose, and **wiggle eyes**.

Penguin Bank

By Edna Harrington

1. Cover an **oatmeal container and lid** with black **felt**. Ask an adult to cut a coin slot in the lid.

2. Trace the bottom of the container onto **thin cardboard**. Add feet to the circle. Cut out the shape, and cover it with felt. Glue the feet to the bottom of the container.

3. From felt, cut out a beak, a belly, wings, and a scarf. Glue them on. Add **wiggle eyes**.

4. For earmuffs, twist two **chenille sticks** together. Glue a pair of felt circles onto each end. Glue the earmuffs to the penguin's head.

Make a Perky Penguin Puppet

By James W. Perrin, Jr.

1. To make the penguin's body, cut two egg cups from a **cardboard egg carton** and glue them together. Be sure to line up the outside edges of the cups so that they form a solid front for the penguin. The hole in back will be for your finger.

2. Cut wings and feet from egg-carton scraps.

3. Paint the penguin's body and wings black, and paint the feet orange.

4. When the paint has dried, glue the wings and feet onto the body.

5. Glue a **cotton ball** to the front of the penguin for a stomach. Glue on **wiggle eyes** and a beak cut from **colored paper**.

Knit Pick

Follow each person's yarn to see what he or she is knitting.

Winter Word Hunt

The twenty winter words below are hidden in this frosty snowman. To find them, look up, down, across, backward, and diagonally, but always in a straight line.

```
        T   J   V   E
      E   A   C   H   F
    X   I   Z   H   R   V
      L   Q   Z   Z   O
      S   L   D   E   S
      R   H   E   O   T
    A   T   O   J   V
    K   M   J   A   A   E
  S   F   L   W   B   R   L   L
S   N   L   S   T   A   O   O   F
    I   O   X   E   R   Q
    K   W   T   F   V   I
    Z   S   C   F   R   R
    X   T   W   I   I   E
  O   A   I   O   T   D   F
  C   N   S   S   L   R   F
  I   T   I   S   L   E   D
  W   O   N   S   T   D
  O   B   O   O   T
  D   L   O   W
  P
```

BOOT	FIRE	HAT	SKATE	SNOW
COAT	FLAKE	ICE	SKIS	SNOWBALL
COLD	FORT	PLOW	SLED	WIND
DRIFT	FROST	SHOVEL	SLEET	WINTER

Now, can you find the boot, coat, knitted cap, shovel, skate, sled, and snowplow hidden in this picture?

Can you find these 12 items hidden in this winter scene?

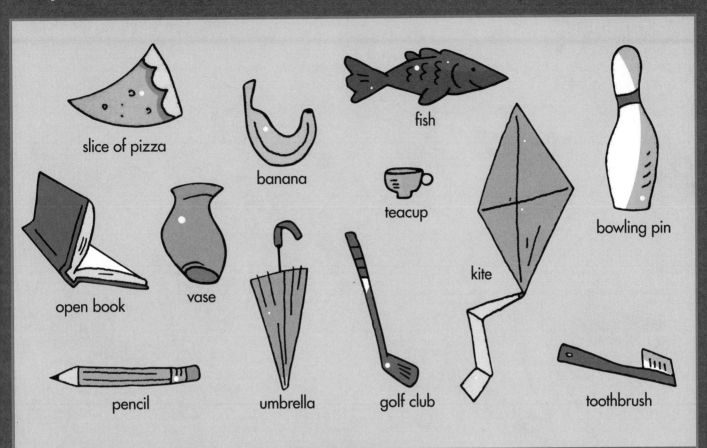

slice of pizza

banana

fish

bowling pin

open book

vase

teacup

kite

pencil

umbrella

golf club

toothbrush

Dot to Dot

Connect the dots from 1 to 28 to see something else fun to do on a winter day.

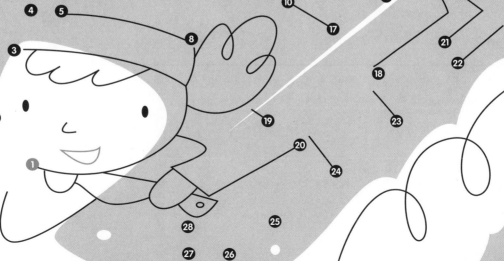

Snow Business

Jack made his best—and funniest—creation out of snow ever.
What do you think Jack built? Draw it here.

Illustrated by Mike Moran

Silly Sliding

Illustrated by David Coulson

Game Q's

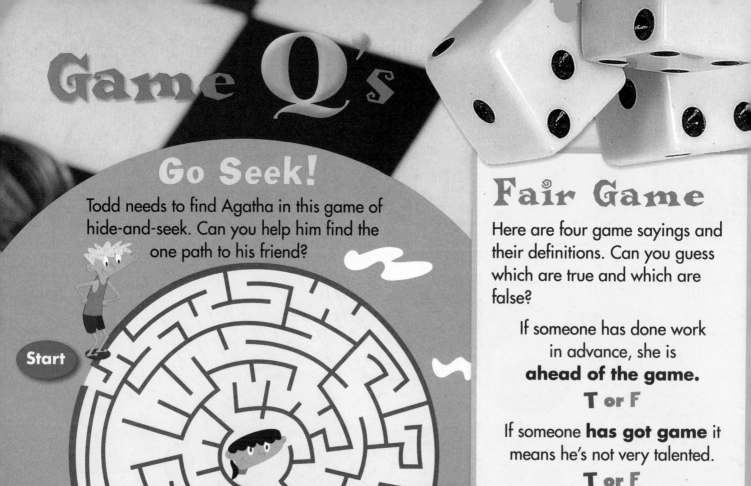

Go Seek!

Todd needs to find Agatha in this game of hide-and-seek. Can you help him find the one path to his friend?

Start

Fair Game

Here are four game sayings and their definitions. Can you guess which are true and which are false?

If someone has done work in advance, she is **ahead of the game.**

T or F

If someone **has got game** it means he's not very talented.

T or F

If a store is **the only game in town**, it means it has mini-golf.

T or F

If someone has a **game plan**, he has a strategy in place.

T or F

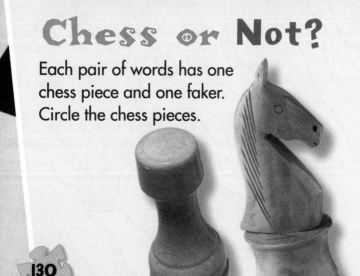

Chess or Not?

Each pair of words has one chess piece and one faker. Circle the chess pieces.

Queen or Princess?

Kook or Rook?

Bishop or Cardinal?

Peon or Pawn?

Knight or Knave?

Jester or King?

Game Designer

Your friend is starting a board-game company and wants you to design the first game. Draw it here!

Missing Vowels

GM is the word *game* with the vowels taken away. Can you figure out the names of these five gms?

TG

HRSSHS

HPSCTCH

FLLW TH LDR

CPTR TH FLG

A Pair of Jacks

Two of these jacks are exactly the same. Can you find the matching pair?

Puzzles by Carly Schuna

Illustrated by Mike Moran

131

Hidden Pictures®
Baking Cookies

teacup

hairbrush

handbell

toothbrush

worm

egg

paper clip

banana

dragonfly

fish

light bulb

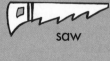
saw

pencil

crown

ice-cream cone

Illustrated by Tim Davis

132

5 Ice Team

The MVP is number 35.

6–7 Cool Crossword

Across
3 BOOTS
6 SCARF
7 EVERGREEN
9 REINDEER
11 PENGUIN
13 HAIL
16 POLAR BEAR
17 SNOW

Down
1 IGLOO
2 FROST
4 SKATE
5 ICEBERG
8 NORTH POLE
10 BLIZZARD
12 ICICLE
14 WALRUS
15 MITTENS
16 PLOW

9 A Winter Walk

12 Tic Tac Row

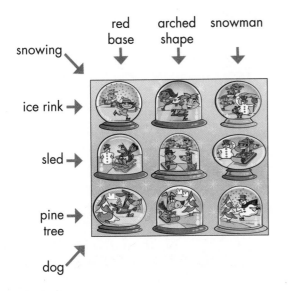

snowing

red base   arched shape   snowman

ice rink →

sled →

pine tree →

dog →

8 The Puck Stops Here

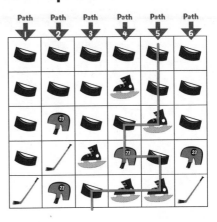

Path 1   Path 2   Path 3   Path 4   Path 5   Path 6

10–11 Alaska Q's

Doggone It!

Moose Watch

True or Not?
1. False (It was the 49th.)
2. True
3. True
4. False
5. True

Jumbled Animals
wolf
seal
salmon
grizzly bear
bald eagle

City or Not?
Anchorage
Fairbanks
Juneau
Nome
Sitka

13 Letter Drop

What do you call a flamingo at the North Pole?
A BRRRD

Answers

14–15 Get Down

Why don't mountains get cold in the winter?
THEY WEAR SNOW CAPS.

18 Square Off!

SNOWMAN   ICE-CREAM CONE

ICE POP   ICICLES

These are all cold things.

20–21 To the Top

First place: Nate—9 hours, 40 minutes
Second place: Jeanine—9 hours, 50 minutes
Third place: Brad—10 hours

22 Skate Pond

23 Dot to Dot

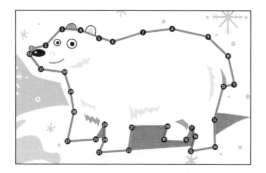

It's a polar bear!

24 Penguin Path

25 Downhill Run

Trudee: $5 - 6 + 4 + 3 + 7 - 2 + 1 = 12$

Mara: $-3 + 6 + 4 + 2 + 7 - 5 - 1 = 10$

Jean: $7 - 4 + 5 + 3 - 6 + 2 + 1 = 8$

Herb: $6 + 3 + 2 - 5 - 7 + 1 + 4 = 4$

Trudee wins!

26–27 Hockey Search

32 Slippery Slope

33 Stuck in the Ice

1. RICE
2. DICE
3. NICE
4. MICE
5. TWICE
6. SPICE
7. SLICE
8. PRICE
9. JUICE
10. VOICE
11. ADVICE
12. POLICE OFFICER

34–35 The 🔑 to It All

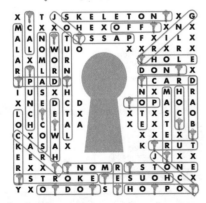

Where do locksmiths go on vacation?
THE FLORIDA KEYS

36–37 Match Maker

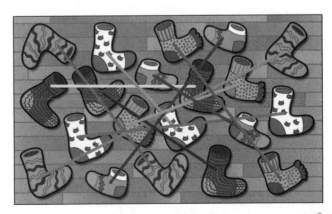

Answers

38 Snow Problem

House lot—200 feet long
Parking lot—700 feet long

39 Double Fun

40–41 Snow Day!

42 Tapping Time

43 Dot to Dot

It's a bird with a leaf!

44–45 Wiggle Pictures

46 Precise Ice

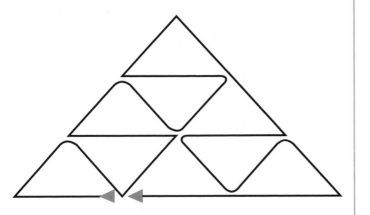

47 Plow a Path

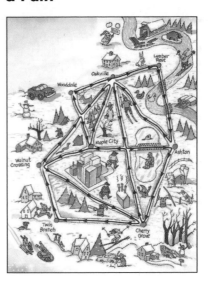

48–49 Twice the Ice

50–51 Snow Ball

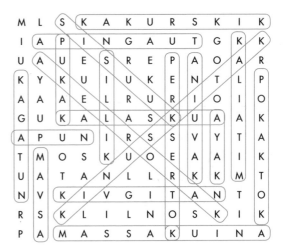

52–53 Knit It

54 Snow Way!

Simon: sweater, $35

Nora: art supplies, $30

Oscar: basketball, $25

Wanda: video game, $50

Answers

58 Wheee!

59 Dot to Dot

It's a snowman!

61 Hockey Hunt

62–63 Time for a Nap

64–65 Weather Q's

Snow Tread

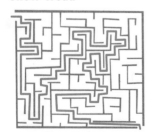

It's Raining, It's Pouring

B and C are exactly alike.

Weather Words

Here are some words we found. You may have found others.

get	log	met	more	tee
greet	lore	meteor	ore	toy
leg	meet	mole	role	yet
let	melt	moor	room	yore

Weather Quiz

1. True

2. False. The world's highest recorded temperature was in Libya: 134 degrees Fahrenheit in 1922.

3. False. It was -128 degrees Fahrenheit recorded in Antarctica in 1983.

4. False. It was recorded in Australia at 253 miles per hour.

Cloud Gazing

NIMBUS, CUMULUS, and STRATUS are the clouds.

Answers

70–71 Flake Search

72–73 Snow Kidding

74 Baby Bear Riddle

Why were the baby bears cold, even under the warmest quilt?

THEY SLEPT IN THEIR BEAR SKIN.

75 Dog Sleds

76–77 Slide to the Finish

78–79 Match Maker

Answers

80 The Right Route

81 Mental Blocks

Here are the answers we got.
You may have thought of others.

P	A	N
I	C	E
G	E	T

B	O	O
O	U	R
A	T	E

S	T	A	R
T	A	L	E
E	L	S	E
P	L	O	D

82 Pile It Up

83 Dot to Dot

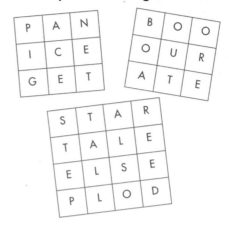

It's hot chocolate!

84–85 I ♥ Cookies

87 Peak Performance

	271		
	146	125	
71	75	50	
27	44	31	19

88–89 The Amazing Mazers

91 Two of a Kind

90 Waiting for a Nibble

94–95 Arctic Animals

1. CARIBOU
2. ARCTIC FOX
3. POLAR BEAR
4. PTARMIGAN
5. SNOW LEMMING

96 Snow Bears

97 Cookie Code

1. MACAROON
2. LEMON BAR
3. SUGAR
4. FORTUNE
5. GINGERSNAP
6. SHORTBREAD
7. OATMEAL RAISIN
8. PEANUT BUTTER
9. CHOCOLATE CHIP
10. SNICKERDOODLE

What did the gingerbread man
use to trim his fingernails?

A COOKIE CUTTER

98–99 Match Maker

Answers

102 Wrapping Up

Amber: green gift, blue bow
Billy: blue gift, yellow bow
Chad: red gift, green bow
Daphne: yellow gift, red bow

104–105 Heart Search

There are ten red hearts and eleven white hearts, so there are more white hearts.

108 Sleep Walk

103 Bunny Run

106–107 On Ice

109–110 Accidental Memories

What kind of clinic would a lumberjack visit for a toothache?

An AXE-I-DENTAL clinic

111 What's Next?   C-A-F-B-D-E